D1135277

WHEN DID YOU
LAST WASH YOUR FEET?

First published in 1986 by
André Deutsch Limited
105 Great Russell Street London WC1B 3LJ

Copyright © 1986 by Michael Rosen
Illustrations copyright © 1986 by Tony Pinchuck

ISBN 0 233 97859 3

British Library Cataloguing Publication Data

Rosen, Michael, *1946 –*
    When did you last wash your feet?
    I. Title   II. Pinchuck, Tony
    821'.914   PR6068.068

ISBN 0-233-97859-3

Printed in Great Britain by
R. J. Acford, Chichester, Sussex

André Deutsch

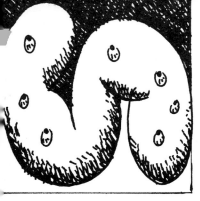

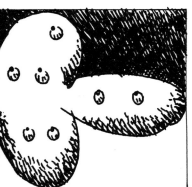

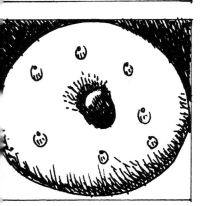

Spots
I gottem

As soon as one goes down
another comes up

Spots
I gottem

They say you gettem
if you don't wash
They say you gettem
if you eat chips
They say you gettem
if you stay indoors

Spots
I gottem

I've washed eight times a day
eight days a week
Spots
I gottem

I eat carrots 'stead of chips
Spots
I gottem

I stand out of doors
let the rain beat my face
Spots
I gottem

I tried medicated soap
tubes of cream
jars of paste
lotions
potions
sprays and foams

Spots
I gottem

Maybe it's my skin's fault
My skin's gone mouldy.
There's an upper layer
that's gone rotten
and a lovely lower layer
that just can't get through

yep
Spots
I gottem

So I scraped my skin
with pumice and luffa
hard towels
and dry flannels

O yes
Spots
I gottem

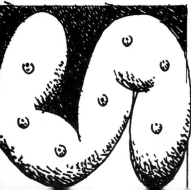

Then I discovered pores.
wow
pores
holes in your skin.
They get blocked up, man,
blocked up with muck
and your face can't breathe.
Your face is supposed to breathe?

Mine doesn't.
Spots
I gottem

Un
clog
each
pore
with steam
antiseptic
steam

So I stuck my face
over bowls of
steaming salt water
till my eyes boiled.

Spots
I still gottem.

Dad says
when I was your age
I never got spots
Mum says
when I was your age
I never got spots

But me
Spots
I gottem

Maybe it's my blood.
It's too thick
or too thin
or too sweet
or too sticky.
Maybe it's trying to get out
bubble up
it's too hot
bubbling up
like volcanoes
and it bursts out to get cool.

oh yes yes yes
Spots
I gottem

My face is covered with
volcanoes
my skin
can't hold
the hot blood
in

yes
you've guessed it
Spots
I gottem
and I've gottem
and I've gottem.

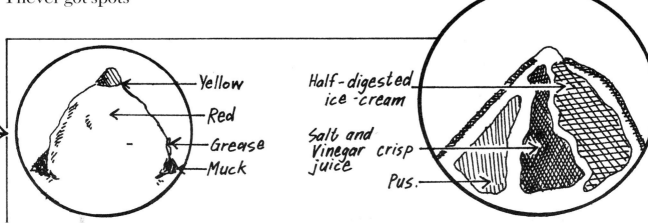

Yellow
Red
Grease
Muck

Half-digested
ice-cream

Salt and
Vinegar crisp
juice

Pus.

PARENTS'

SAYINGS

I was mucking about in class.
Mr Brown said:
'Get out and take your chair with me.'
I suppose he *meant* to say:
'Take your chair with you.'
So my friend Dave said:
'Yeah – you heard what he said:
'Get out and take my chair with him.'
So my friend Ken said:
'Yeah – get out and take his chair with me.'
So I said to Mr Brown,
'Yessir – shall I take our chair with you, sir?'
Wow.
That meant

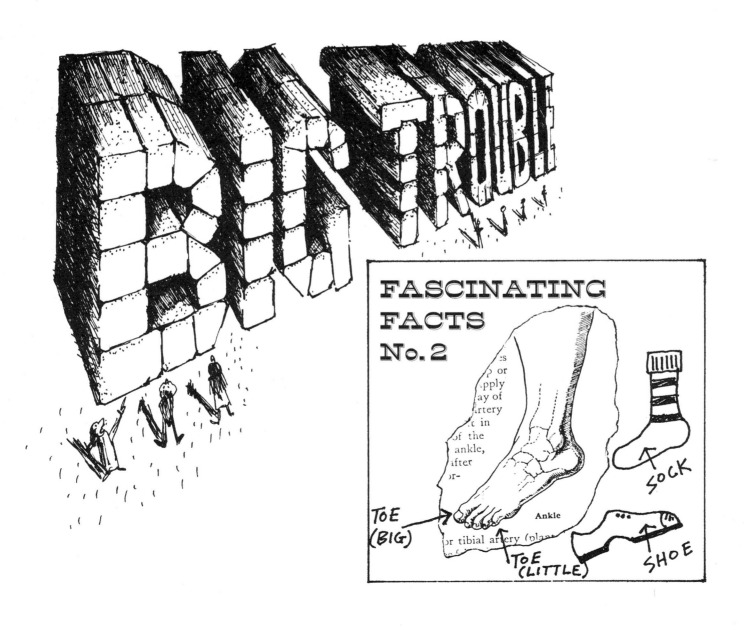

FASCINATING FACTS No. 2

TOE (BIG)

TOE (LITTLE)

Ankle

SOCK

SHOE

TRAFFIC NEWZ

Wonderful Bee Bee Cee
tra – ff – ic newwwwws
over now to Scotland Yard
with Bob Gunk.

"Well, things aren't looking too good
at the moment.
There's been an accident at Chiswick Flyover.
A car is blocking the road
under the flyover
after a herd of moles
dived off the flyover
on to a blue Ford Cortina.

Over the other side of London
there's trouble at Tower Bridge.
The Bridge was closed at a quarter to six
this morning
but it was not possible to open it.
to let HMS Corgi through
as no one could remember how to do it.
They tried shouting,
'Open Sesame, Open Ali Baba, Open Pickled Onion,'
but nothing worked.

Any commuters driving on the River
are advised not to, because their cars will sink.

That's it from me."

ICE CREAM

At home,
when we had ice cream
we'd all sit round eating it
going
'Mmmm, this is nice. This is really nice.'
But then my dad'd say,
'You know what this could do with?
Just a little bit of fruit salad with it.'

So next time we had ice cream
we had ice cream
and
a little bit of fruit salad with it,
and we'd all sit round eating it
going,
'Mmmm, this is nice, this is really nice.'
But then my dad'd say,
'You know what this could do with?
Just a few chopped nuts on the top.
That would really make this perfect.'

So next time we had ice cream
we had ice cream, a little bit of fruit salad
and
a few chopped nuts over the top,
and we'd all be sitting round eating it
going
'Mmmmm, this is nice, this is really nice.'
But then my dad'd say,
'You know what this could do with?
A few of those
little tiny bits of chocolate
scattered over the top
that would make it –'

But my mum wouldn't let him say anymore.
She goes,
'You're always the same, you are.
Nothing's good enough for you, is it?
I'll tell you something –
if you don't like this cafe
find another one.
You know why you're like this?
I'll tell you.
It was that grandmother of yours
It was her fault.
She pampered you.
You were pampered, you were.
All I ever hear is,
"No one makes it like my grandmother did."
Well you can get this into your head.
I'M NOT YOUR GRANDMOTHER. OK?'

And my dad'd turn to us and go,
'What did I say?
What did I say wrong?
All I said was,
'A few little bits of chocolate
over the top would be very nice.'
What's wrong with saying that?
A few bits of chocolate
would be very nice, wouldn't they?
What's all the fuss about?
What   is   all   the   fuss   about?'

QUOZZ

I had a party.
I asked over
Monkie, Stoll, Willzie, Rad,
Cheeps, Trio, Staff,
Nellie, Rich, Tails
and O.Vee.
But I didn't ask
Quozz.
I didn't ask Quozz
'cos I didn't really like Quozz
and I don't think Quozz liked me.

Every so often he'd have a go at me.
He'd try and get my blood up,
stick a ruler in my ribs
nick my bag –
the usual stuff.
I tried to stay cool
but every so often
I'd lose my temper
and we'd be rolling round the ground
punching, groaning,
sweating, swearing,
until the others:
Monkie, Stoll, Willzie,
Rad, Cheeps, Trio, Staff,
Nellie, Rich, Tails and
O.Vee
separated us.

A DAY IN THE LIFE OF QUOZZ

8.00 A.M. DO PRESSUPS, BULLWORKER, CHEST EXPANDER, WEIGHTS ETC...

URRGA!

So I didn't really like Quozz
and I don't think Quozz liked me.

So I didn't ask him to our party,
did I?

At this party
we had hot dogs and beans
and told jokes.
Nobody said, 'Where's Quozz?'

Nobody said, 'Why isn't Quozz here?'
Nobody said, 'It's a pity you didn't ask Quozz'.

Somewhere a few miles away,
I suppose Quozz was sitting on his own
thinking,
'They're all up there at Rosie's place,
they're all having a fantastic time
and Rosie hasn't asked me.'

Now as it happens
this party was at Easter
and it was the Easter Quozz left school.
So come the new term,
Quozz wasn't there.
But every so often one of the others'd
meet him.

Monkie met him at the bus stop
at the bottom of the hill
and Quozz came up to Monkie and said,
'Look, Monkie, if you see Rosie,
tell him if he's coming down the hill sometime
and I'm here
I'm going to bash his head in.'

Rad met him outside the barber's
and Rad came in to school and said,
'I met Quozz
and the first thing he said to me was,
'Tell Rosie,
if he's coming down the hill sometime
I'm going to be there
and I'm going to bash his head in.'

Then Trio came in one day
and said he'd met Quozz
and Trio said Quozz said to him:
'I'm going to hire a hall
and I'm going to get in my brother's band

and they're going to do Little Richard numbers
and Stevie Wonder
and Chuck Berry
balam bam boola
balm bam boola
tutti frooty
all night long in their white suits
and I'm going to ask everyone
all the blokes
and all the girls too
except Rosie.
He's not going to come.
and if he turns up at the hall
trying to get in,
I'm not going to let him in.
And if you see him
tell him,
if he comes down the hill sometime
and I'm here
I'm going to bash his head in.'

AFTER LUNCH: LEARN MORE BOASTS.

I PUT BACK 8 BOTTLES OF BARLEYWINE LAST NIGHT. WAS I CUT!!

I THREW AWAY MY SNAKESKIN SHOES.

AFTERNOON: WALK THE STREETS DOING NOTHING.

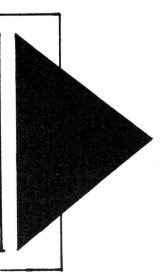

Not long after this,
I was bowling down the hill
to the bus stop
and suddenly – there he was
Quozz
he comes up to me
and he's standing there
Next to me.
And he goes,
'Hi, Rosie,'
and I go, 'Hi, Quozz'
and he stamped his feet a bit,
he sniffed
breathed on his fist
and said, (very casual)
'Taters, i'n' it?'

'Taters? Taters?' I said, 'What's that?'
'Taters in the mould, cold, it's rhyming slang,
don't you know nothing?'

So I go,
'Oh is it? Is it? I didn't know.'
'Yeah. It is.'
'How's things then, Quozz?' I said.
'Great,' he said.
'How's things with you?' he said.
'Great', I said.

LATER: KICK CAN INTO ROAD.

KERINK

REST OF AFTERNOON: STARE INTO
WINDOW OF MOTORBIKE SHOP.

VROOM
VROOM!
VRRRM!

He hung about for a bit
swinging his arms around
and then off he went
down the street on his own.

I didn't see him again
and I've never seen him since.

Anytime I ever hear anyone say
'taters'
I think of Quozz
and I think
why didn't I say to him,
'Did you hire the hall
and did you get in your brother's group
in their all white gear?'

Why didn't I say,
'Hey, Quozz,
are you going to bash my head in now
or later?'
But I didn't.

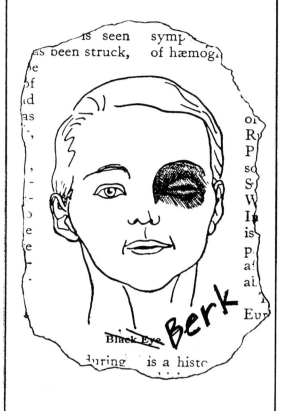

No. 1 The Berk

TRIO

Once I went out with a girl in my class.
Then I stopped going out
with this girl in my class.
Then my mate Trio
went out with this girl in my class.
Then my mate Dave
said I was an idiot.
'Why?' I said.
'Well,' he said.
'because when you went out with her
Trio says you said to her
you'd been waiting for this for a long time.'
'What's wrong with that?' I said,
'What did I do wrong?'
'Look,' said Dave
'You should never show a girl that you're grateful.'
'Why not?' I said.
'It shows you're weak,' he said.
'Oh I see,' I said.

But I didn't see.
I didn't say that I didn't see
in case that would show I was even more weak.

NIGHTMARE

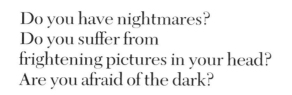

The Giant Spider is back
and crushing everyone in sight.

Industrial waste pumped into the sea has produced a
living mass of sludge.
The creature rampages through the city
destroying everything.

Terror unleashes on a small American Town
when thousands of worms are driven to a frenzy
by an electric storm.
They turn on the inhabitants
and start eating them.

Nice.
They'll put an end to all those nasty dreams
you've been having
won't they?
Will they?
Won't they?

When I went to the new school
people noticed I was a Jew.

I was the only one.

So they did the jokes:
you know,

throwing a penny on the floor
to see if I'd pick it up

rubbing their noses

going 'my boy' and 'my life'
while they were talking to me.

And if ever I had to borrow any money
there'd be uproar,
cheering, jeering,
'Don't lend him any money, you'll never get it back.'

Sometimes I'd go along with it
and I'd put on what I thought was
a Jewish voice
and say things like
'Nice bit of schmutter.'

It's like I was bringing Zaida
my mother's dad, into the playground
running round him going,
'You're a Jew, you're a Jew.'

'It's like I was saying,
'Yes, I'm a Jew
but I'm not like other Jews,
I'm an OK-Jew.'

But I wasn't.
For them I was just
Jew.

I was the Jew that it was
OK-to-say-all-the-foul-things-
you-want-to-say-about-Jews-to.

And I played along with it,
I thought it'd stop them hating me
but all it did
was make it easier for them
to hate all Jews.

WE'VE ONLY GOT ONE BLACK KID IN THE SCHOOL SO WE DON'T HAVE MUCH PREJUDICE HERE.

THAT'S WHAT YOU THINK, PIG!

PLAYGROUND

I'm in the house
Susanna's in the garden.
The baby is in the pram.
Joe is next door.
The sun is out. It's hot.
Suddenly, there's the sound of chanting:
'Paki, Paki, Paki, Paki.'

It's kids
on the playground out the back.

Susanna's peeping through the fence.
I'm standing on a chair.

A bunch of boys are moving in
on the swings, jeering.
Four women in white are retreating,
taking children with them,
taking them away from the swings.
Four women in white shawls.

Susanna is shouting, 'Trouble!'
I'm off my chair,
out the door, into the sun,
and out on to the playground.

An eight-year-old
has a crushed coke can in his hand.
He is going to hurl it.
I grab the railings:
'You – hey you – put that down.'

The chanting stops.
The playground stops moving.
Every eye is on me.
A few legs dangle from the swings.

Over by the roundabout,
two mothers and a dad
sit tight.
It's nothing to do with them,
it seems.
There is a total silence among
a hundred people.

Some words of a speech
come into my head
and next moment I'm shouting:

Maybe I shouted:
'We don't want filth like that here,'
Maybe I shouted:
'Keep filth like that off this playground.'

They look at me.
'He started it,'
one of them says.

'He did not,' says one of the women in white.
'I did not,' says the boy, her son.
Then the four women in white
draw together and retreat
taking their children with them.

Refugees,
driven off playground swings.
For a moment I am helpless
I can't stop this sad retreat.
I can see I may have stopped
someone being hurt
I can also see, I can in no way
then and there make those swings
become a nice place to be
for the sons and daughters of the four women
in white.

One of the mothers
who had sat on the wall by the roundabout
comes near.
She looks down at the boy
who was going to hurl the can:
'You're a liar,' she says.
'You picked on them,
the moment they come on to the playgound.'

He seems proud of it.
The retreat goes on.

'Next time I'll smash your head in,'
says one of the can throwing mob
to one of the refugees.

So I say,
'They've as much right to be here as you.'

The women and children
walk out through the gates
their silks blowing as they walk.

'They live and work here, right?'
I say.
So the one who promised to smash the boy's head in,
says, 'Why should we have to change our laws
for them?
They don't even try to behave like us.'

So I say,
'Why should they have to behave like you?
Mind you,
The way you behave – it's a good thing they don't.'

'I'm going,' he says.

The swings are swinging again,
people are saying nothing,
taking sides in their heads; the sounds and pictures of the
day
turning into reports and stories
over their tea in an hour's time.

'I'm going after them,' says
the wild boy with the crushed coke can.
This time it's a bottle.
He turns to the one who
wants them to behave like him:
'I'm coming with you,' he says.
'Oh, no you're not,' comes the reply.
'I'm going home. You go on your own,
seeing as you think yourself so hard,'
he says.

I take that as a sign:
he is not totally horrible.
But –
The swings have been captured
the women and their children have gone.
I stand on the corner of the playground
and my eyes fill with water.
I check it.
I dry them.
I go indoors
and tell Susanna my tale.

A hundred others will be doing the same later.
As I walk back I wonder what they will say about what
they have seen.

Susanna says,
'The women gave as good
as they got, you know.'

I thought she meant words –
throwing back their words at them.
She meant coke cans.
While I ran round the block to get in to the playground,
she saw a Bangladeshi woman
all-in-white,
her arm raised to hurl that coke can back.
That's her tale.

That night
me and those hundred people
can settle down and watch telly.
It's comedy time on Thames TV.

A man is acting being an idiot.
He starts talking about Pakis.
Pakis with bandages round their heads.
He meant turbans.
But the man didn't know better –
because he was supposed to be an idiot.
An Irish idiot. That's entertainment
On TV – for us.

Every so often an Indian,
a Bengali or an Asian is killed
on the streets of London.

Every so often
British TV comedy script-writers
write jokes about Irish idiots
and Pakis with peculiar habits.
Entertainment for all the family
on TV tonight.

Comedy for everybody –
except the human race.

Killingly funny.

SPELL IT.

We didn't used to have
POETRY
in our class
we used to have
SPELLING
instead.
Each week, every Friday,
the teacher used to write up 12 words
on the blackboard
and she'd say

LeaRN THEM!

Then we had to write them down
in our notebooks.

You didn't have to know what the words meant.
You didn't even have to know how to say them.
All you had to know was how to spell them.

There was the word

sepulchre

I was always sure it was said
SEPP-ULL-KREE.
I still don't know what a sepulchre is.

So come the next Friday
she rubbed all the words off the board
and she goes:

YOU!
(pointing at you)
HOW DO YOU SPELL SEPULCHRE?

And you sat there going

errr...errr...

WHAT'S IT BEGIN WITH, FOOL?

err...S?

THEN?

errr...I?

NO, FOOL.

YOU BOY, WHAT COMES NEXT?

I don't know.

WHAT? BUT YOU'VE HAD A WHOLE WEEK TO LEARN IT.

I had to see the doctors, miss.

EVERY NIGHT?

No miss.

You just felt terrible.
Each week, every Friday,
you sat there.
Would the finger be pointing at you?

Friday morning
on the way to school
A,
S,
P,
er
(quick glance at the notebook)
A,
R,
er
(quick glance at the notebook)
A,
G,
A no I mean U. U?
(quick glance at notebook)
yes U
S
ASPARAGUS
into school
The finger.
YOU BOY

Oh no…
here we go again.

Then she gave us
DICTIONARIES…wow.

and once
me and Harrybo
we were going through it for rude words…

But they weren't there.
I mean it was
'NELSON'S FIRST DICTIONARY'.
Dark blue cover.
And it just didn't have the words in
none of them.
So there we were giggling over
a word that was in
that wasn't rude
but if you read it another way
it could be rude…
And she saw us
and she goes,

I HOPE YOU TWO ARE NOT LOOKING UP SOMETHING INDECENT.

No, miss,
says Harrybo,
we're laughing
over an old joke.

GOOD,
she says, glaring.

She was dead good at glaring.

And I was thinking

she's going to come over
and look at the page
and find out
and it will be a rude word
and we'll really get it.

Nelson's
1st Dictionary
(CLEAN)

I glanced down at the page
and I saw
KISS

so I thought

if she asks, what word?
I'll say,
we were looking up KISS
(because that's sort of nearly rude, isn't it?)

But she believed Harrybo's story about the old joke.

GOOD

she says

and went off
still GLARING.

I think she thought words are OK
so long as all you do is spell them.
What starts getting really messy
is when people find out
what words mean...

BEFORE & AFTER

Before I was alive
I wasn't anywhere.

I wasn't inside a mother
I wasn't a voice in the dark
I wasn't a movement in a room
I wasn't in a locked box
I wasn't under a pillow

I was utterly nowhere
I had no place
no space
no mark
no beginning
there was no me
there was only a nothing

and the nothing
was full of other people
who didn't even know
that I was a nothing.

When I die
I won't be anywhere
I will give myself
to medical students
to cut up into bits
so that they can try and remember
where the bits go

and then they can throw the bits
in a bin
and burn the bits
and send the ashes off
to somewhere they're filling
in a bit of wet land

and then again
I won't be inside a mother
I won't be a voice in the dark
I won't be a movement in a room
I won't be in a locked box
I won't be under a pillow

I'll be utterly nowhere
I will have no place
no space
no mark
no beginning
there will be no me
there'll only be a nothing

and the nothing
will be full of people
who won't even know…
No!
who *might* know…
who?

MASTERCLASS: *Geography*

40   ~~PARTY GAMES~~

Fig. 4. For Long Distance Flights you need a map and some cardboard aeroplanes. The player making the flight is blindfolded.

he breaks off abruptly—like a serial story. His neig ...
with the ...ve, doing h...

FASCINATING FACTS
No. 2,357

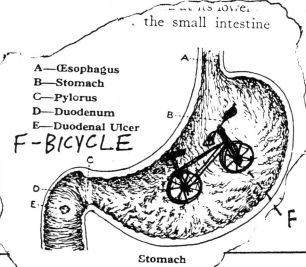

... at its lower ...
... the small intestine

A—Œsophagus
B—Stomach
C—Pylorus
D—Duodenum
E—Duodenal Ulcer
F—BICYCLE

Stomach

...m) through

Last week
I went to my old school.
I used to go there about 25 years ago.
It was a kind of big party
for anyone who'd ever been to the school.
I didn't know who I'd see.
That awful guy Quozz
who sat on Trio's chest
and hit Trio's mouth so hard
that his tooth came through his lip.

Ron?
He was in our end of the world ceremony
that we held on the school field
when we all dressed up with our jackets inside out
and ties round our heads.
The head wrote in my report after that:
'I don't mind him celebrating the end of the old world
I hope he enters the new one a little more soberly.'

My mate Monk?
Who used to sit in the back of lessons
doing impressions of Louis Armstrong
and doing drum solos on his knees.

Maybe
my old girl friend Sharon
would be there.
That had started one Christmas
after school one night
and she came walking towards me
across the classroom
with a twig of mistletoe in her hand
saying:
'You know what you do under the mistletoe,
don't you?'
We did.

Or Cherry?
She organised a petition
all round the school
saying
we had to be allowed to use the hall
to put on the play.
She drove her dad's landrover
and had two enormous dogs.

And then teachers?
Maybe Mr Latham
who said to me,
'We should've been on the side of the Germans
in the last war.'
Which,
considering some of my family
died in German concentration camps
wasn't a great thing to say.

Mr Carroll
the woodwork teacher
who watched me take a whole year
to make one leg of a stool.

Or maybe Miss Bell?
Who once ran out of our class
crying
because while she turned round to the blackboard
the whole class put on paper hats
so when she turned back to the class
we were all sitting there
grinning like idiots
with all the hats on our heads.

Well,
Quozz, Ron and Monk weren't there.
Cherry wasn't there.

Sharon was there,
she works for some kind of Charity
saving dogs in Egypt.

Mr Latham's dead
Mr Carroll's dead
Miss Bell's dead

so they weren't there.

Mr Duffy
was there.
He said to me:
'You've come on a bit
since you were in my geography lessons,'
So I said,
'Most of the time I wasn't *in* your geography lessons.
I was outside the door, wasn't I?'
And he didn't think that was very funny at all.
But then he's a headmaster now.

Howard was there
who said that Dave Simons,
who once drew a picture of the chemistry teacher
with his head
peeping out of a lavatory bowl
was now teaching art at
my other old school.

Jean Mitchell was there.
She tried to get me to believe in God and Jesus.
She married Graham
and they first held hands
by the gym
when they were eleven, would you believe?

Anyway,
there was this group of us
killing ourselves laughing about
this time Sid Williams
was caught exposing himself at the back of class.
Mr Davis had said:
'Don't think I don't know what you're doing, boy.
Come out here.'
And Sid didn't even have time to
put it away . . .

Then while we were remembering this,
Liz Hackett
who's a teacher now
said to me:
'You know when you were at school
I hated you.
I don't think I've ever hated anyone
as much as you.
You were the most horrible person
I've ever known.
You were foul
you were cruel
I really hated you, you know.'

Wow.

People breathed in and out
for a bit.

I kind've went
well, yeah, I suppose so.

Then the little group of us
broke up
and we went off in various directions
for the rest of our lives.

'And the next call is from Anne in Purfleet.
Hallo Anne'

'Hallo – can I speak to the psychologist please?'
'Yes go ahead, Anne, he can hear you.'
'Hallo, Anne.'
'Hallo.'
'What's your problem?'
'I don't know where to start really. You see,
my husband had an affair
eighteen months ago.
He didn't tell me.
I just found out.
He said he had to be in Brighton
on a job one weekend
but he wasn't.
I found this letter when I was
sending his jacket off to the cleaners.
It was from her.
Now he has promised me
he'll never see her again,
but I don't trust him.
Everytime he says he'll be late
or he's got a job to do somewhere
I think of this woman.'

'But he's promised you, hasn't he?
Don't you believe him?'

'Oh yes, I believe him
but I just can't get it out of my mind
that it could happen again.'

'Have you spoken to him about it?'

'Just once.
But he said he didn't want to talk about it.
It was all water under the bridge.'

'There you are, then.'

'Pardon?'

'It's all past and forgotten.
If you're still worried about it,
talk to him.'

'I can't.
You see my husband doesn't talk,
and he refuses to talk about this.
He says it's all in my mind.'

'It is, isn't it?'

'I suppose it is really.'

'You see
aren't you over-reacting on this.'
I don't think you've sorted yourself out, have you?
I think you've got to come to terms
with him
with yourself
and face up to the reality of the situation,
haven't you?
Mm?

'Yes, Thank you.'

'Is that all right, Anne?'

'Yes'

'Anything else?
Thanks for your call.'

If all we had to do was
simply become more and more skilful
then we could admire and applaud
the craft and brilliance
of the engineers and fence-builders
the plumbers and welders
the fitters and designers
the draughtsmen and the architects
the planners and the chemists
who made Concentration Camps
the clever places they were.

The Dead Man in Euston Station

What with
him lying in the middle of Euston station
at the top of the stairs,
they stopped the escalator
in case we bumped into him
or something,
so when we got to the top of the stairs
we filed past him

gawping at his face

it was grey.

The nurse was pile-driving his chest
and a black oxygen mask
was hissing like air-brakes do
when lorries stop at the lights.

Some of us stopped to watch.

There was his shoes to look at.
Polished this morning.

There were the medics to watch
heaving all the apparatus around.

There was death to look at
and we haven't all seen that,
have we?

Seen plenty of pictures of it
Falklands, Beirut, Northern Ireland
Seen plenty of mock-ups of it
Julius Caesar, cowboy films.

So we hang about
to get a look at
how it's done – dying.
How someone else does it.

But of course
no one's going to say
things
like:
"He's doing
it very well."
"I'll try that when I do it."

No one's thinking:
"Huh, when it came to it
he mucked the whole thing up.
I won't."

No one's thinking:
"When I do it
I'll do it better."

It all seems like it's
a mistake
like he made a
mistake

what with him
lying in the middle of Euston station.

THE ROW

in our "GUESS WHO'S TALKING" series

with: ken & Mandy

A: SOMETHING'S THE MATTER.
B: NO IT ISN'T.

A: THEN WHAT ARE YOU SULKING ABOUT?
B: I'M NOT SULKING.

A: WHAT'S THE MATTER?
B: NOTHING.

A: WELL YOU'RE NOT EXACTLY HAPPY ARE YOU?
B: I'M ALRIGHT.

A: YOU DON'T LOOK IT.
B: I DON'T HAVE TO SHOW IT.

A: YOU USED TO
B: SO NOW I DON'T

A: YOU'RE TELLING ME.
B: YES I KNOW I'M TELLING YOU.

A: SOMETHING'S THE MATTER THEN.
B: NO IT ISN'T.

A: YES IT IS.
B: WELL IF YOU KNOW SO MUCH ABOUT ME YOU DON'T NEED ME TO TELL YOU.

NO I SUPPOSE NOT. I'LL BE OFF THEN. I'LL SEE YOU WHEN i SEE YOU...

THE PINNER VILLAGE STOMPERS

You probably haven't heard of a band
called the Pinner Village Stompers.

This was before Soul, Punk,
New Romantics, Lovers Rock, and Dub.
It was the time of Trad Jazz Clubs
like The 100 Club and Klooks Kleek
and Big Production Companies were flying in
old black musicians from New Orleans
like Kid Ory.
They were re-releasing Jelly Roll Morton and his Red Hot Peppers,
and the English groups of the day
were led by people like Chris Barber.

The Pinner Village Stompers only did one gig.
March 8th 1962
Spare room round at my place.

Amongst us lot there was Dave, who could play St Louis Blues on the piano
there was Rad
who could play the clarinet
there was Monk who could play nothing
Trio who could play nothing
and me who could play nothing.

LIVE TONIGHT
AT THE SPARE ROOM

So we said,
let's get together on Sunday
and have a 'session'.
When they came over
we all piled into the spare room.
Rad got out his clarinet.
There was no piano so Dave was on comb and paper.
Dave brought some drum sticks
which he lent to Monk
but we didn't have any drums
so Monk was on cardboard box.
Trio said Alex Welsh used Maraccas
so he was on coffee tin and drawing pins
and I was on nail-file stuck in side of table.

Then my brother came in and said
he could play the recorder.
Dave said,
'For godsake, you don't have recorders
in jazz bands.'
But Rad said it was OK
because we were a bit short on solo instruments
and Dave said
if we had a piano he could play St Louis Blues.

Then we said to Rad, 'What are we going
to start with?'
And he said,
'Petite Fleur.'
Then I said, 'Hold it. We could tape it.'
'Fantastic idea.'
And I set the machine up
and we were away.

DRAWING PINS IN COFFEE TIN

Fender DRAWING PINS IN COFFEE TIN

NOW WITH DOLBY C, D +E NOISE REDUCTION.

MORE...

CLARINET

SUITABLE FOR MOST PURPOSES

RECORDER

BETTER THAN NOTHING.

COMB & PAPER

USEFUL FOR BEGINNERS

Clarinet, recorder, comb on paper
cardboard box, coffee tin and drawing pins
nail-file in side of table.

When we got to the end
Dave said, actually,
my brother wasn't too bad on recorder
and we all said Rad
was fantastic.
Then we played it back

It didn't really sound like
King Oliver and the Hot Seven
So Monk put his sunglasses on.
And Trio said,
anyway, we didn't have a name.
A name!
What name?

Dave said we could be the Fifth Form Footwarmers
but no one wanted to bring school into it.
Someone said it should be something to do with Rad
like Rad's Jazzmen.
Someone said we owed it all to New Orleans anyway
so it should be something like
Rad and his New Orleans Hot 5.
In the end we all agreed on
The Pinner Village Stompers.

Then we 'cut' the 'next track'.

Rad played 'Tiger Rag'.
Dave was great on comb and paper.
Monk on cardboard box and sunglasses
made it feel kind of classy.
Trio really shook those drawing pins
in that coffee tin.
I pulled that nail file
something wild.
And my brother played the recorder.

Then we played it back.
Our first track as The Pinner Village Stompers.

Then Monk said,
'What one shall we do now?'
Rad said he only knew 'Petite Fleur' and 'Tiger Rag'
but if *we* wanted to play something on our own
we could.
Dave said
if we had a piano
he could play St Louis Blues.
and Monk said, 'You know something, Dave?'
'What?'
'If we had a piano you could play St Louis Blues'.
and Dave said, 'I know,
I know I could,'
and Monk fell about laughing

So we played back both numbers again.

The soaring clarinet
the wailing recorder
the gutsy comb-and-paper
the urgent cardboard-box-and-sunglasses
the biting coffee-tin and drawing pins
and the – well – the nail file
and what could you say about that nail file?

Then we called it a day.

What with one thing and another
we never got it together again.
Dave took up drumming on classroom tables,
Monk bought a pork pie hat,
Trio met Pat Boone at the Church of Christ Scientist.
Rad played Mozart in the school orchestra.
My brother went out and bought a geological hammer.
There'll never be another band like it.
Sunday March 8th 1962
Spare room round at my place.

Historic.

CARDBOARD BOX

GOOD FOR OUTDOOR GIGS.

NAIL FILE IN TABLE

A "NO-SWEAT" INSTRUMENT.

SUNGLASSES

INDISPENSIBLE.

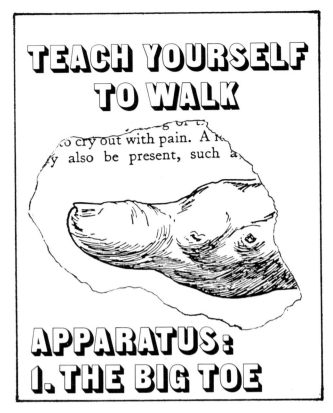

TEACH YOURSELF
TO WALK

...o cry out with pain. A ...
...y also be present, such a...

APPARATUS:
1. THE BIG TOE

When I was Fifteen

Ken said to me,
'You know your trouble,
you don't hold your bag right.'
'What's wrong with it?' I said.
'It's not so much the way you hold it –
It's the way you put it down.
You've got to look at it as if you hate it.
Watch me.'

He went out
he walked back in
shoulders back
elbows out
bag balanced in his hand.

'Watch me.'

He stopped walking.
His arm froze
and the bag flew out of his hand
as if he'd kicked it.
He didn't even look at it.
'Now you try,' he said,
'and I'll show you where you've gone wrong.'
I went out the door,
I ambled back in again with my bag.
I stopped walking,
my arm froze – just like his,
but the bag fell out of my hand
and flopped on to the floor
like a fried egg.

'Useless,' he said,
'You don't convince – that's your trouble.'
'So?' I said,
'I'm a slob. I can't change that.'

I didn't say that I *would* try and change
in case that would show I was giving in to him.

But secretly,
on my own,
in my room,
in front of the mirror,
I spent hours and hours
practising bag-dropping.
Walking in,
freeze the arm,
let the bag drop.
Walk-in
arm freeze
bag drop.
Again and again
till I thought
I had got it right.

I don't suppose any girl noticed.
I don't suppose any girl ever said to herself,
'I love the way he drops his bag...'

PERFECT YOUR BAG-DROP TECHNIQUE WITH *Ken*

① THE GRIP.

② THE TESCO KNEE-LIFT.

③ THE OUTWARD THRUST MARKS AND SPARKS DROP

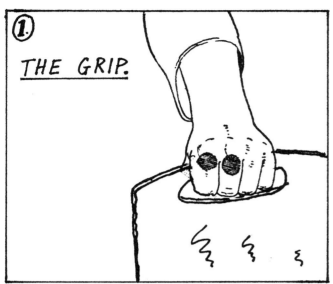

④ THE WICKED SAINSBURY ARM-FREEZE.

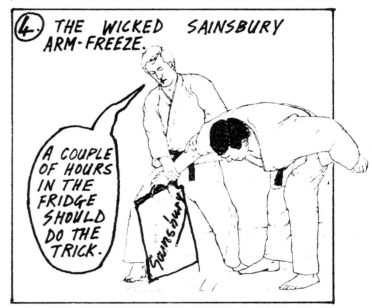

⑤

⑥

Doodle

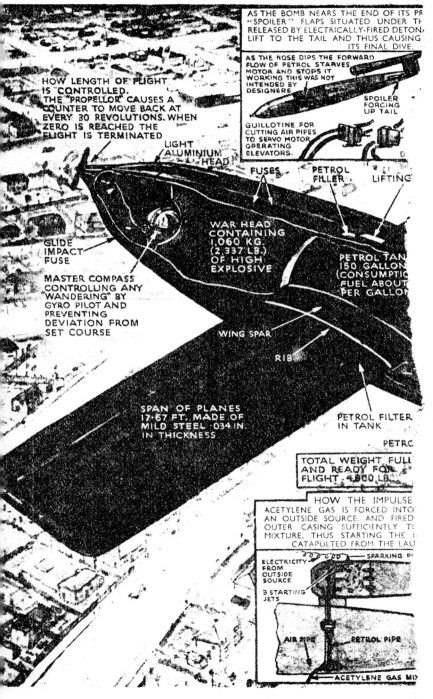

HOW LENGTH OF FLIGHT IS CONTROLLED. THE "PROPELLOR" CAUSES A COUNTER TO MOVE BACK AT EVERY 30 REVOLUTIONS. WHEN ZERO IS REACHED THE FLIGHT IS TERMINATED

LIGHT ALUMINIUM HEAD

GLIDE IMPACT FUSE

MASTER COMPASS CONTROLLING ANY "WANDERING" BY GYRO PILOT AND PREVENTING DEVIATION FROM SET COURSE

FUSES

PETROL FILLER

LIFTING

WAR HEAD CONTAINING 1,060 KG. (2,337 LB.) OF HIGH EXPLOSIVE

PETROL TAN 150 GALLON (CONSUMPTIO FUEL ABOUT PER GALLON

WING SPAR

RIB

SPAN OF PLANES 17·67 FT. MADE OF MILD STEEL ·034 IN. IN THICKNESS

PETROL FILTER IN TANK

AS THE BOMB NEARS THE END OF ITS PR "SPOILER" FLAPS SITUATED UNDER TH RELEASED BY ELECTRICALLY-FIRED DETON LIFT TO THE TAIL AND THUS CAUSING ITS FINAL DIVE.

AS THE NOSE DIPS THE FORWARD FLOW OF PETROL STARVES MOTOR AND STOPS IT WORKING THIS WAS NOT INTENDED BY DESIGNERS

SPOILER FORCING UP TAIL

GUILLOTINE FOR CUTTING AIR PIPES TO SERVO MOTOR OPERATING ELEVATORS.

PETRO

TOTAL WEIGHT FULL AND READY FOR FLIGHT 4,800 LB.

HOW THE IMPULSE ACETYLENE GAS IS FORCED INTO AN OUTSIDE SOURCE. AND FIRED OUTER CASING SUFFICIENTLY TO MIXTURE, THUS STARTING THE I CATAPULTED FROM THE LAU

ELECTRICITY FROM OUTSIDE SOURCE

SPARKING P

3 STARTING JETS

AIR PIPE

PETROL PIPE

ACETYLENE GAS MI

GERMAN FLYING BOMB. This is a small automatic, steel-constructed aircr The power unit consists of a thin metal tube, open at the rear but closed at the fro shutters. On the launching ramp, acetylene gas is fed to the tube from outside an The mixture heats the tube and the bomb is then catapulted off at 180 m.p.h. b action (see lower and top right-hand insets). The aiming of the bomb is achieve

Sometime after
baked beans on toast
sometime before bathtime
you could say,
'What was it like, Mum?'
'Were you scared, Mum?'
And she always had time,
made time,
to say.

She had a whole world war
to explain,
she was there
after all.
'What was it like, Mum?'
'Were you scared, Mum?'
'You see,' she said,
'you'd see rockets in the sky
called doodlebugs
and so long as you could hear
this doodlebug you knew
it wasn't going to land on you.

But then the sound in the sky
would stop.
Count 10.
We'd count
and the doodlebug
would drop
and a bomb went off.

The silence of a doodlebug in the sky.
We were scared then.

bug

Once I came out of White City Station,'
she said,
'nearly dark.
No lights allowed.
Half a mile from home
in the White City flats.
They said to us

"If the sound in the sky stops –
LIE DOWN IN THE GUTTER."

Lie down in the gutter,
I ask you.
What a thing to say.'

'Did a doodlebug drop then, Mum?
Did it?'

'No'.

'What happened then?'

'Nothing.'

'Oh, Mum. Something must have happened.'

'No. Just that.
Walking through the streets in the dark
thinking over and over and over

"Will I have to lie down in a gutter
tonight?"'

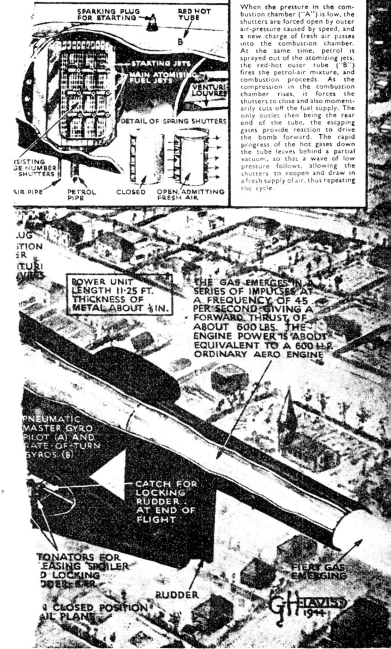

THE WORKING
IMPULSE MOTOR EXPLAINED

SPARKING PLUG
FOR STARTING

RED HOT
TUBE

B

STARTING JETS

MAIN ATOMISING
FUEL JETS

VENTURI
LOUVRES

DETAIL OF SPRING SHUTTERS

RESISTING
GE NUMBER
SHUTTERS

AIR PIPE

PETROL
PIPE

CLOSED

OPEN, ADMITTING
FRESH AIR

When the pressure in the combustion chamber ("A") is low, the shutters are forced open by outer air-pressure caused by speed, and a new charge of fresh air passes into the combustion chamber. At the same time, petrol is sprayed out of the atomizing jets, the red-hot outer tube ("B") fires the petrol-air mixture, and combustion proceeds. As the compression in the combustion chamber rises, it forces the shutters to close and also momentarily cuts off the fuel supply. The only outlet then being the rear end of the tube, the escaping gases provide reaction to drive the bomb forward. The rapid progress of the hot gases down the tube leaves behind a partial vacuum, so that a wave of low pressure follows, allowing the shutters to reopen and draw in a fresh supply of air, thus repeating the cycle.

UG
STION
ER
TURI
VRES

POWER UNIT
LENGTH 11·25 FT.
THICKNESS OF
METAL ABOUT ⅛ IN.

THE GAS EMERGES IN A SERIES OF IMPULSES AT A FREQUENCY OF 45 PER SECOND GIVING A FORWARD THRUST OF ABOUT 600 LBS. THE ENGINE POWER IS ABOUT EQUIVALENT TO A 600 H.P. ORDINARY AERO ENGINE

PNEUMATIC
MASTER GYRO
PILOT (A) AND
RATE-OF-TURN
GYROS (B)

CATCH FOR
LOCKING
RUDDER
AT END OF
FLIGHT

TONATORS FOR
EASING SPOILER
D LOCKING
DDER BAR

RUDDER

FIERY GAS
EMERGING

G H DAVIS
1944

CLOSED POSITION
IL PLANE

l air: the height of travel is also pre-set and is controlled by an aeria
e drives a shaft whose revolutions are counted, measuring off exactly
hed, the bomb is pushed into its final dive by the use of electrically fired
situated in the tail planes and so lift the rear of the robot (see top left
is is reproduced here by courtesy of the "Illustrated London News."

BODYWORK

I have just discovered
a hole in the floor of my car.
I say, '*my*' car.
It was my mother's.
She died and my dad said
I could have it.
The hole in the floor is
rust.
You know what they say about rust,
don't you?
Rust in the bodywork of a car.
You've got to stop it early on,
before it gets a grip,
before it spreads through the whole car
and it just falls apart;
the engine can fall out
or you can get into the car one day
and stick your foot through the floor
or a door's hinges can get eaten up
and the door can come away in your hands.
It doesn't take long, they say,
from the time you first spot it
to the time you might just as well junk it.
Two years say – or two hard winters.
So I suppose I'd better do something about
my mum's old car.
Mum died of cancer.

DINNER Time

They used to say
we couldn't stay in school
during dinner time.
So we had a plan.

Sixteen of us went up
to the monitor on duty
and told her that we had
to move some chairs for the caretaker.

So she let us in
and then we went to our room
and picked up one chair each,
and off we went
in single file
each holding a chair
like a conga.

And we walked all round the school.
We went through the dinner hall
along the corridor
across the playground
back into school
past the head's office
and every now and then
we'd say,

HEAD

'We're just moving these chairs
for the caretaker, sir.'

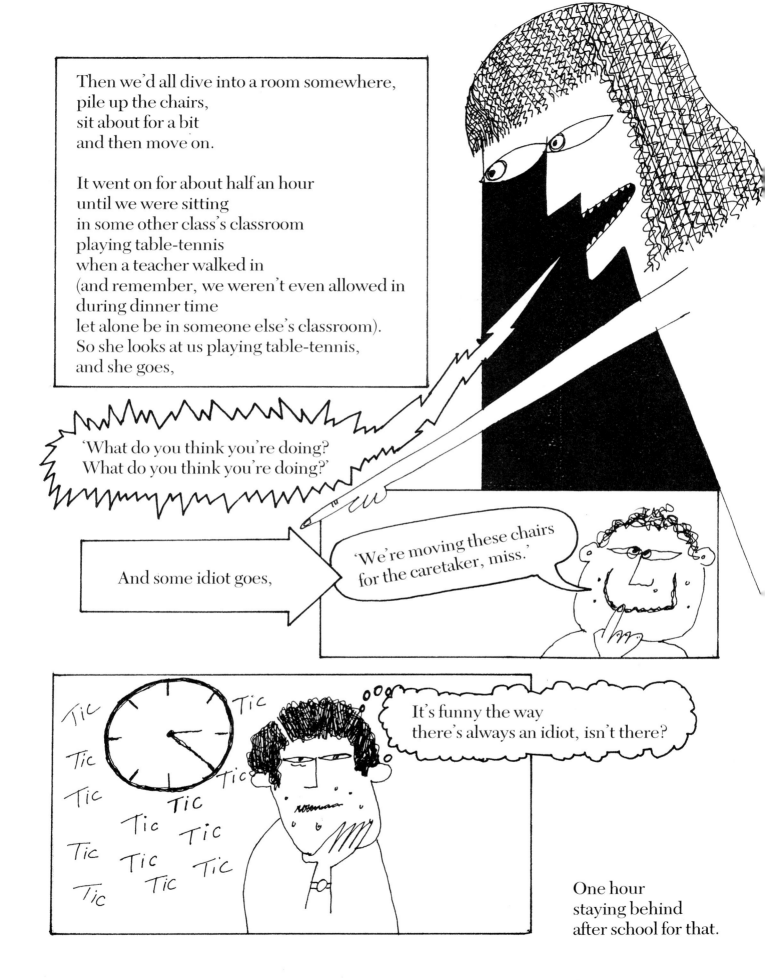

Then we'd all dive into a room somewhere,
pile up the chairs,
sit about for a bit
and then move on.

It went on for about half an hour
until we were sitting
in some other class's classroom
playing table-tennis
when a teacher walked in
(and remember, we weren't even allowed in
during dinner time
let alone be in someone else's classroom).
So she looks at us playing table-tennis,
and she goes,

'What do you think you're doing?
What do you think you're doing?'

And some idiot goes,

'We're moving these chairs
for the caretaker, miss.'

It's funny the way
there's always an idiot, isn't there?

One hour
staying behind
after school for that.

Mr H.

Richard Royce and Linda Jones
used to lean against the wall by the gym.

They were told
        not to stand
        so close together.

They used to hold hands by the fence.

They were told
        not to touch each other.

They used to stand at the bus stop
with their arms round each other.

And so they were told to
        leave each other alone.

In the dinner time
they used to climb over the fence
and go into the woods down there.

We all knew.

        Once Mr H. saw them nipping over there.

What we heard
was that he went and followed them in there,
pulled them out
and had them chucked out of school.

        Richard Royce and Linda Jones never came back.
        They were
        Expelled.

Someone said that
Mr H. said
he had never been so disgusted by what he had seen there
In All His Life.

Mr H.
was the cleanest person I've ever known.
His shoes were incredible.
So was his hair.
In fact,
His hair and his shoes were the same.
Very very shiny.

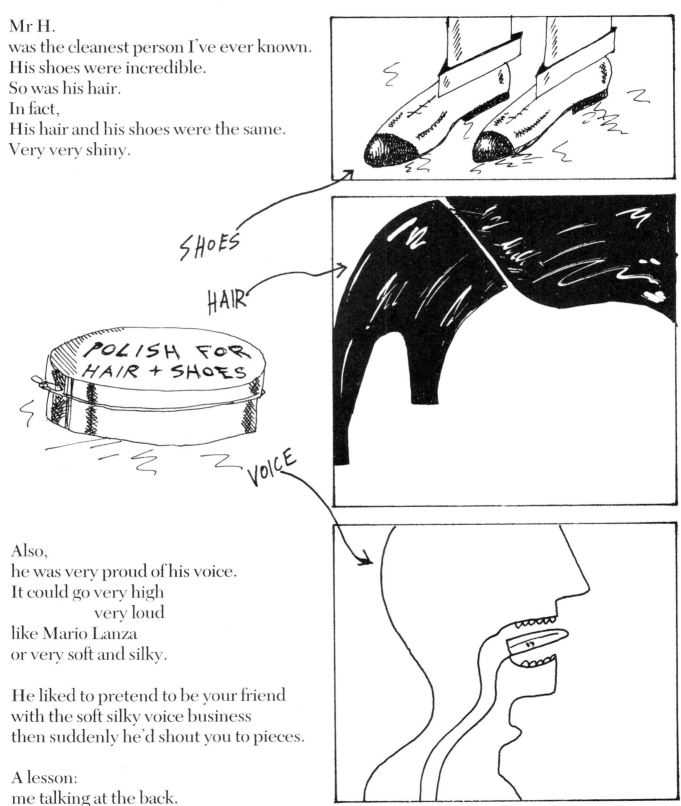

SHOES

HAIR

POLISH FOR
HAIR + SHOES

VOICE

Also,
he was very proud of his voice.
It could go very high
              very loud
like Mario Lanza
or very soft and silky.

He liked to pretend to be your friend
with the soft silky voice business
then suddenly he'd shout you to pieces.

A lesson:
me talking at the back.

Soft voice and smile:

'Are you receiving me, Rosen?'

'Yes sir.'

Then he yells:

WELL I'VE HAD ENOUGH OF YOU BOY IS THAT CLEAR?

And you're sitting there with your ears shattered.

The man was totally right about everything.
He was the kind of person
who, when he looked at you,
he made you feel your neck was dirty.

Some girls had a crush on him.
He looked like a photo from an old film
a kind of
wing-commander brain-surgeon.

Anyway,
he expelled Richard Royce and Linda Jones.

Twenty years later
I met a woman
who had been at school with me
and I was asking her about
Quozz and Lynne and Kay
and suddenly she said,
'Did you hear about Mr H.?'

'What?'
'He got chucked out.
Suspended for "professional misconduct".'
'What did he do?'
'You remember Miss S., the gym-teacher?
He got caught with Miss S.
After school.
They were at it in the medical room.
He got chucked out.'

I couldn't believe it.
Him –
in his dark blue suits.

I wonder what Richard Royce and Linda Jones
would think of that if they knew…

In the Playground

In the playground
at the back of our house
there have been some changes.

They said the climbing frame was
NOT SAFE
so they sawed it down.

They said the paddling pool was
NOT SAFE
so they drained it dry.

They said the see-saw was
NOT SAFE
so they took it away.

They said the sandpit was
NOT SAFE
so they fenced it in.

They said the playground was
NOT SAFE
so they locked it up.

Sawn down
drained dry
taken away
fenced in
locked up.

How do you feel?
Safe?

FUN
PROHIBITED

NOT
SAFE

NAFF IDEAS
NO. 1 : THE SCHOOL DISCO

let's write the NEWSPAPERS

YEAH, LET'S

Expert says Nuclear war will only kill 99% of us

PC 83 SAVES FLY'S LIFE

Three-year-old saves Granny with deadly karate chop

Mass murderer's axe in auction for Save the Children's fund

The president of Ladbrokes on Mars, who today offered odds of 1,000 to 1 against an honest politician being discovered.

Duke of Edinburgh's barber in dog smuggling racket

MI5 man leaked next week's Dallas script to the Russians

Roman coins find in pensioner's baked beans

Newspaper apology:

We apologise to the Director of Sparks and Menders.
The interview with him
that we printed in yesterday's paper
in which he was reported as saying
'When I'm really happy
I eat Sparks and Menders Jumpers'
was completely made up by us.
We never have interviewed the Director of Sparks and Menders
and we probably never will now.
We've been asked by the director of Sparks and Menders
to pay him two million pounds damages
or eat Sparks and Menders crispy fried Haddock chunks
for the next twenty years.
The two million pounds has been paid.

DINGO!
Join our "Win an Australian dog" competition

ALL THE THREES 33 ROWRF!

We were once at a party
and there was this really big bloke
called Arnold,
and he had on a big thick white jumper
with a collar that went up under his chin
and he had this really big belly
that stuck out over the top of his trousers.

At the party
he was talking in a really loud voice
and you could hear him all over the house.

Arnold knew about everything.
Someone said
they had a tap that dripped.
Arnold knew all about taps,
Arnold knew all about drips.

Someone said they had heard a story
that came from Jamaica.
Arnold knew all about stories,
all about Jamaica,
all about Jamaican stories,
all about stories about Jamaica.

Arnold knew all about everything
and you could hear him all over the house.

In the middle of all this,
I noticed that
down the front of Arnold's big thick white jumper
was a great big stain.
Like someone had poured coffee over him
or he had left his jumper
lying in dog food.

Ever since this party
whenever one of us has a mark
on a jumper
we say,
'Oh look – you've got an Arnold on your jumper,'
Or if there's a stain on the carpet
we go,
'Oh no – look at this mess
there's a great big Arnold on the carpet.
I'll never be able to wash it off.'

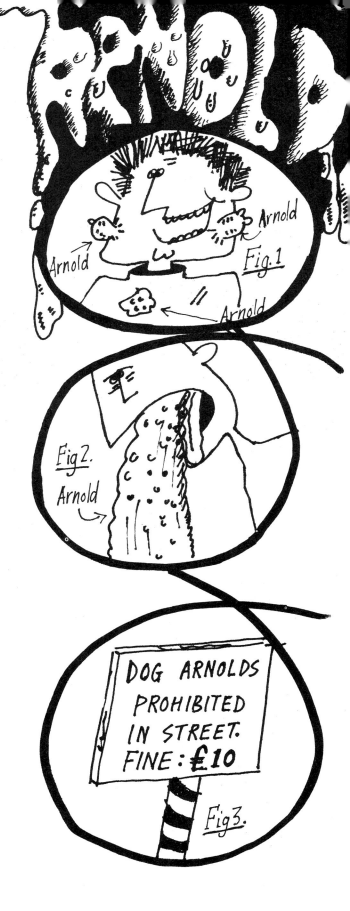

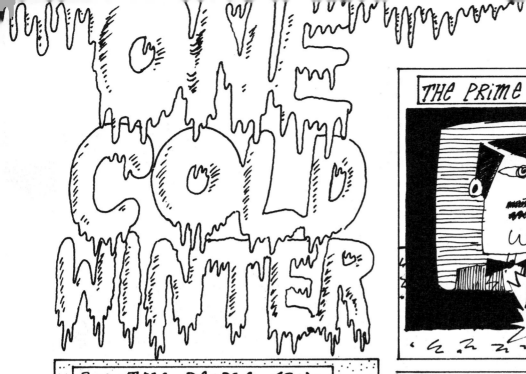

SCHOOLS CLOSE...

FACTORIES CLOSE...

HOSPITALS CLOSE...

and BABIES DIE.

SO THE POOR PEOPLE BECAME AFRAID OF THE ANGER OF THE RICH PEOPLE. AND THEY WENT BACK TO WORK...

BETTER!

FACTORIES CLOSE THINGS BETTER

TIMES SCHOOLS CLOSE BABIES DIE

BACK TO WORK HOSPITALS CLOSE

TELECRUMT LOWER WAGES BETTER FOR ALL SAYS PM.

BUT SCHOOL'S STILL CLOSE, FACTORIES STILL CLOSE AND BABIES STILL DIE.

AND THE POOR PEOPLE STILL STOP WORKING. THOUGH NOW, IT'S WHEN THE RICH PEOPLE STOP THEM WORKING.

YOU'RE ALL FIRED!

THE RICH PEOPLE SAY:

WE CAN'T AFFORD TO HAVE SO MANY SCHOOLS

So many FACTORIES

So many HOSPITALS

So many BABIES

SOME POOR PEOPLE THINK:

WE CAN'T AFFORD TO HAVE SO MANY RICH PEOPLE.

SOME PEOPLE THINK:

WE CAN'T AFFORD TO HAVE ANY RICH PEOPLE

Maths

We were sitting in maths.
Room eleven
sun streaming in through the windows
blackboard covered in hundreds of tiny numbers.
(If he wrote his numbers bigger
there'd be a chance you could understand
some of it)

The door opens.
It's the secretary
with a new bloke.
He's going to be in our class.

Stare stare whisper whisper.

Sandra Wilson and Diane Rose look at him.
It looks like they think he's amazing.
Really nice.
Diane Rose is Jewish and Sandra Wilson
wishes she was.
At the moment she's trying to find out
how to convert.

Diane Rose only goes out with Jewish fellers.
Well,
she can only take someone home if he's Jewish
otherwise she'll get it in the neck
from her dad.
Her mum as well, actually.

So,
she says, if she fancies a non-Jewish boy
she keeps it to herself
and tries to forget
about him.

Anyway,
mostly she goes to Jewish clubs
so it doesn't often crop up.

Except in school.

And Diane Rose says she can tell
if someone's Jewish.

So the new feller walks in
right in the middle of maths.

Sandra Wilson and Diane Rose
are pretty excited about it.
Sandra Wilson opens her eyes up
and she starts to speak
without making a sound,
across the room
to Diane Rose.

'Jew-ish?' mouths Sandra Wilson.
'Who? Him?' mouths Diane Rose.
Sandra Wilson nods.
Diane Rose stares at him.

She looks back at Sandra Wilson.
'Ye-es. Ye-es.' Big nodding.
She's certain.

Maths teacher stands up.
'Right you can stop working.'
(It's alright, we hadn't started.)

'We've got a new boy,
joining us as from today.
His name is
Sanjay Patel.'

Diane Rose looks at Sandra Wilson.
Sanjay Patel?
That's no Jewish name...

Sanjay told us later
his old man was Indian
wanted him to do well in exams
so he wasn't going to muck about
or nothing.

Later,
well – about three weeks later
Diane Rose and Sanjay
started going out together.

This ought to prove something...

Mum

When mum was dying
some people came
some stayed away

some people came and saw
her grey face

some people came and saw
the hole in the side of her head
but some stayed away

some sat and talked
some brought her old books
some saw her fingers drumming
but some brought nothing
because they didn't come

sometimes I met them
in the street
in other people's rooms
getting into cars

always the same
'How's Connie?'

What held them away
from our door?
Was it the dark rooms?
The rows of bottles of tablets?
The heavy scent of her perfumed cushion?
Or the sight of her shiny skin
stretched over the bones of her skull?

They kept their distance
they kept her in her place
they left her for dead
months too soon.

THIS IS IT

When I visit schools
and people want to say
do you want to go to the toilet
they never say
do you want to go to the toilet
they say things like

Do you want the geography?
The usual conveniences are just down there.
If you need the cloakroom it's . . . no? OK.
If you want to spend a penny it's next to the staffroom.
The men's is at the top of the stairs.

Bathroom? Mmm?

GEOGRAPHY

BATHROOM MMM?

COR!
DROOL
DRIBBLE
DROOL
DRIP
PORNBOY

wAr

A group of eight-year-olds
follow me into a room.
Three boys, three girls.
'Let's move the table,' I say.
We all move the table.
'Who's going behind the table?' I say.
'Me,' says one boy –
'Gettaway from the girls,' he says.

After eight years alive in this world
we have taught him to be at war
with half the people in the world.

CLASSROOM

Quite often
you sit with your back to the teacher
you bounce a ping-pong ball on the table
you practise breaking your mate's neck
you beat rhythms on his back
you sit on top of the cupboard
you climb out of the window.

Sometimes
you notice there's a teacher in the room
and he or she says,
'Now I would like you to answer the questions on the
board.'
Then you throw a ball of paper at the wall
you yell your mate's name three times
you break your mate's pencil up
you stick the broken pencil in your mate's ear
you throw your mate's pen in the bin
you try smacking the top of your head
    and rubbing your belly at the same time
you fall off your chair
you say,
'If frozen water is called iced water
    what do you call frozen ink?'
'er . . . iced ink?'
'Ugh . . . YOU STINK!'
You say:
'Humpty Dumpty sat on the wall
Humpty Dumpty had a great fall
All the king's horses
and all the king's men
trod on him.'

The teacher seems to be talking too.
The teacher seems to be talking to you.
The teacher says,
'I've told you what to do – so do it.'
So you say,
'What do you want us to do now, sir?'

So you climb into the cupboard
you climb out of the cupboard
you jam a table into your mate's belly
you nick your mate's bag
you eat his crisps
you say, 'Get lost, earoles.'
The teacher seems to be saying to you,
'Hey. You. Sit on your own.'

So you make Match of the Day noises
you wave your arms in the air
you sing, 'Come on you re-eds
          'Come on you re-eds'
you say, 'If you were living in a bungalow
and you painted the bedroom red,
the bathroom white,
what colour would you paint the stairs?'
'I dunno – blue?'
'No. There aren't any stairs, it's a bungalow.'
You say,
'Knock knock'
'Who's there?'
'Cows.'
'Cows who?'
'No they don't. Cows moo.'
So you bend your mate's ruler backwards.
and forwards.
and backwards.
It breaks.
The teacher seems to be saying to you.
'Report to the Head!'
And you say,

'Why?
'That's not fair,
why pick on me,
what was I doing?'

DEODORANT

Why do they write on the side of deodorants
'FOR UNDERARM FRESHNESS' – Why *'underarm'*?
What's the matter with
'Armpit'?
I mean most of us have got
at least one of them,
They are
NORMAL.

'UNDERARM FRESHNESS'
It makes it sound
like little boys playing cricket.

What I've never figured out about deodorants
though
is where does all the underarm sweat go
once you've blocked up your armpits?
Where does it come out?
Your eyes?
You got sweaty eyes?

You know,
one day they're going to invent a nose deodorant.
Not to stop you being able to smell
to stop – yes –
bogies.
Imagine it.
Up in the morning, in to the bathroom
and a quick psssht psssht up your nose.
FOR NO-BOGIE FRESHNESS.
No no no
they couldn't call it bogies.
They'd have to call it
something like
'That unwelcome little business.'

In fact, there are probably people at this very moment
slaving away in research laboratories
over bunsen burners and test tubes
trying to invent deodorants for anything that
doesn't fit into decent life as it is known.

And there'll be people going around spraying deodorants
all over their bodies
and
on their brains.
Brain deodorant
FOR UNDERSKULL FRESHNESS
Stops your brain smelling.
The police would be issued with it.
Here is the News:
As from tomorrow the police
will be equipped with Disinfectant Water Cannon
and Brain Deodorant.

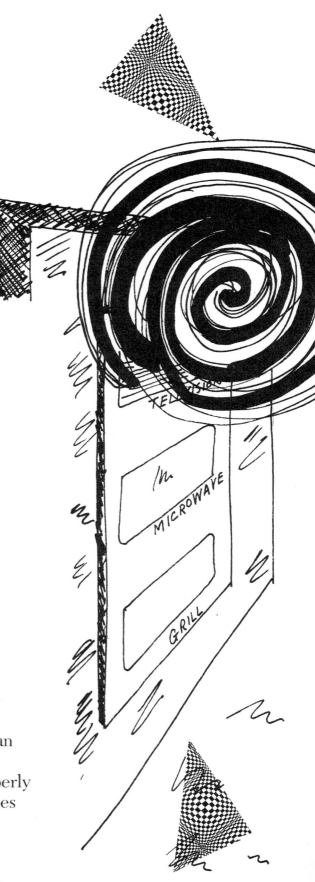

FᴸROM the
fUTURE To the
PᴿESENT

It's the year
1991. *2001*
'Good morning, Home-lovers. Hodeo.
This is your breakfast video.'

The TV panel above the micro-wave oven
and infra-red grill
was spiralling colours:
Indigo, jade, ultra-marine.
Indigo, jade, ultra-marine. *(Every one*
Through the stars and swirls on the screen) *Elisa*
came the painted face of the lead singer
of ZERO'S HEROES, *(Everybody.*
the Intercontinental Orbiting Satellite
Heavy Reggae Funk-Z sound.

'Hi, Home-lovers. Hodeo.
This is your ZERO HERO video.
Hi Hi Hi.'

Elisa
'Oh give over, for gawd's sake,' said a youngish woman
in a silver monkey-suit.
The automatic nappy-softener was not stopping properly
and the aerosol spray was jetting nappy-softener fumes
into the room.

'We used to just boil 'em, rinse 'em
and then put 'em through the mangle,' said someone.

It was a very old frail-looking woman
sitting in what looked like a ball of purple foam.
ZERO'S HEROES moved
and wow
When they moved
they moved
weightless disco, man
swim, guy, swim,
deep deep disco moves.

No one in the room
(that they used to call a 'Kitchen')
watched ZERO'S HEROES.

The woman in the silver monkey-suit
was banging the hell
out of the nappy-softener aerosol dispenser.

'I don't know why the telly
don't have knobs on no more,'
said the very old woman
from her ball of purple foam.

Suddenly
like a razor-sharp axe
cleaving into the young woman's skull
came a picture.
One brief snapshot-frame
that her brain saw
but her eyes didn't.

It was a deep green hillside
It was a vast blue sky
It was a holiday from years before.

It was a slow moving string of boys,
girls, her mates
walking towards a grey slate house.

There was a sound
that her brain heard
but her ears didn't.

'Haloooo
haloooo
haloooo,'
and echoes of friends laughing
laughing in the sun.

And then the whole snapshot,
brain-picture, brain-sound
cut out.

Then the nappy-softener aerosol jammed.
And ZERO'S HEROES
sang,
'Swim, guy, swim
swim, guy, swim.'

'Something the matter, love?' said the older woman
'No I suppose not,' said the younger.

PLANS
in 2 voices

My three year old walks past the building site.
The cabins are high up overlooking the work.
'I wish I was a worker up there,' he says,
'wish I was a worker in a stripey jacket.
When I'm older I'm going to be a worker in a stripey jacket.'

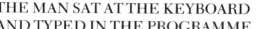
THE MAN SAT AT THE KEYBOARD AND TYPED IN THE PROGRAMME

My three year old says,

'Airplane, airplane, sky,
airplane gone like a bird.
When I'm a big boy I'm going to go to Joe's school.
I'm three.'

'THE MOMENTS BETWEEN
RECOGNITION OF AN ENEMY INTRUSION
INTO EUROPEAN AIRSPACE
AND MISSILE RESPONSE
WOULD BE HANDLED BY THIS PROGRAMME,' HE SAID

He says,

'A 125 is a really speedy train
It's brilliant.
It's speedy.'

HE POURED THE CONCRETE INTO THE
SHUTTERING
TO FINISH THE LAST PART OF THE
SILO.

'Everyone breaks something
sometimes,' says Joe.
'I didn't break the cup on purpose, did
I?' he says.

HE CALCULATED THAT WITH 98.8%
TARGETING ACCURACY
THERE WAS A 97% CHANCE THAT
RUSSIAN SILOS
WOULD BE DESTROYED BEFORE THE
MISSILE INSIDE
COULD BE LAUNCHED.

'WE ARE NOW TALKING IN TERMS OF
WHOLE CITIES SURVIVING ON OUR
SIDE,'

HE SAID, LICKING HIS LIPS.

'We didn't empty the bin in the kitchen
today
so it ponged a bit
and it rained at nine o'clock
just when Tony Blackburn came on.

MASTERCLASS
The Service in Ping Pong

Technique 1:
The Gob Service

THE OPEN UNIVERSITY
COOKERY COURSE

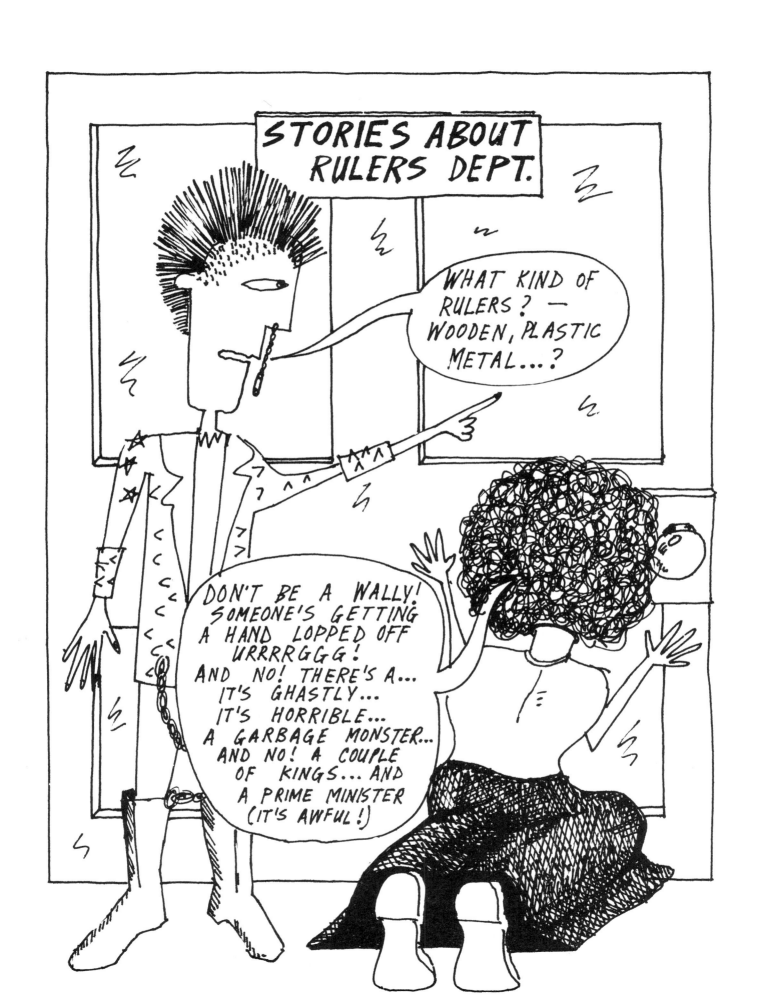

A King Who Promised

Once there was a king who promised he would never chop anyone's head off. He ruled over a very noisy court. Everyone made a noise. They laughed and shouted and sang. They coughed. They hiccupped. They banged and thumped. They booed. They whistled and cheered.

Now, the king didn't like the noise, and he wanted to stop it. So, he thought a bit, and he walked a bit. He thought a bit more – and then he had a plan.

'The next one of you to make a noise will die!' he said.

Everyone went quiet, even though they all knew this king would never chop anyone's head off.

Everyone was quiet – except in one corner, and there was the boy who scrubbed the pots and pans in the kitchen. He was new to the court, and he made a noise and laughed. He liked noise.

The king looked at him. Everyone looked at him. He laughed again.

'Boy! Leave the hall!' the king said.

So the boy picked himself up and went off to the kitchens.

'Guards!' the king shouted. 'Lock the doors!'

The guards locked the doors. The king sat and waited. The court sat and waited. Outside, the boy banged his saucepan and sang.

> *Up and down,*
> *Up and down,*
> *Tim Tom Tackler*
> *Goes up and down.*

A whole hour went by. Not a sound came from inside the hall. Dinner time came, and still everyone was quiet. But outside they could hear the boy's song.

> *Up and down,*
> *Up and down,*
> *Tim Tom Tackler*
> *Goes up and down.*

Everyone was quiet, and now they could hear the boy eating. They could hear the sound of a ladle hitting the big soup cauldron. Like a great bell it was. They heard the soup go slosh into his bowl. They heard him sipping at his spoon. And the ones nearest the door heard the soup gurgling in his belly.

Still they sat.

They heard the sound of sausages sizzling in the pan. They smelt the sausages. They saw the smoke coming under the door, and the ones nearest the door even heard him sprinkling salt and pepper on them.

Still they sat.

They heard the sound of a knife cutting cake, the crack of the icing, and the swish through cream. They heard him smacking his lips and licking his fingers, and the one nearest the door even heard him picking up the crumbs.

> *Eat a bit,*
> *Tim Tom Tackler,*
> *Eat a bit*
> *Tackler Tom.*

The people in the court were going mad with hunger. What was the king up to?

Just when it seemed as if everyone was going to burst, the king spoke to the guards.

'Guards, open the doors!'

Then he turned to the court and spoke again.

'You may go,' he said.

Like a great fierce dragon, they rushed out of the hall, down the steps, round the corner, and into the kitchen where the boy was finishing his dinner. And, like one fierce dragon, they leapt on the boy and pulled him apart.

'Dinner, dinner, dinner,' some shouted.

Drink, drink, drink,' others shouted.

Upstairs the king waited.

Soon his court came rushing back.

'We got him,' some shouted. 'We did for him!'

And the king who never ever chopped people's heads off spoke.

'The next person to make a noise will die.'

This time, everyone did as they were told, and they all went very quiet.

THE NEXT ONE TO MAKE A NOISE WILL DIE.

'NOT A WHISPER'

QUIET ENOUGH TO HEAR A PIN DROP

NO NOISE HERE AT ALL

WASTE

CHAPTER 1

Once upon a time
there was a ruler.
He was an expert
he was very clever
he knew all about Science.

Now, he had a heap of rubbish
piling up outside his palace.
So every day he ordered
men to load up all the rubbish
in a boat
and take it out to sea
and drop it into the sea
where it sank down, down
to the bottom
where no one knows what
slides or creeps or swims or what.

Some people said,
'Why do you do that?
Why do you have so much rubbish
that you have to drop it into the sea?'
'Oh, friends,' he said,
'It's not that it's so very much rubbish,
It's just that it's filthy rubbish,
dangerous rubbish
It could make all of us ill
if I left it lying about.
I drop it in the sea
so it'll never be seen or smelt again.'

And then some people said,
'*We* never see it, it's true,
but there must be *something*, down there
that sees it.'

'Oh yes', said the ruler,
'but only a few sea-worms, or sea-bugs
and a few strands of sea-weed.'

'Oh yes,' said some people,
'but who eats sea-worms, sea-bugs
and strands of sea-weed.?'

'I've no idea,' said the ruler.

'Maybe fish eat the sea-worms and sea-bugs
who eat your filthy rubbish.'

'I can't say I feel sorry for fish,'
said the ruler.

'Maybe *you* eat the fish
that eat the sea-worms and sea-bugs
who eat your filthy rubbish.'

'Then so what? So what?'
said the ruler.

And that was that.

CHAPTER 2

Meanwhile down, down on the sea-bed
where the filthy rubbish
slowly slowly drifted down,
the few strands of seaweed grew up strong
among the rubbish
and the sea-bugs and sea-worms
fed on the strong strands of sea-weed,
they grew fat,
grew big,
but great sores and lumps and cancers
grew on the fat sea-worms
and the big sea-bugs.

And the fattest sea-bugs ate the not-so-fat
and grew fatter,
and greater and greater lumps and sores
and cancers grew
on *them*.

Until,
after many, many years
there lived just one
giant, fat, cancerous
monster of a sea-bug.

One day,
it slowly swam
up, up, up
to the surface of the sea,
raised its ghastly, bulging head
above the waves
and saw, far off,
the land of the clever ruler.

And slowly,
it swam for that land
till it reached the shore
where it climbed out
on to the land.

It then strode across the land
towards the ruler's palace.

Meanwhile,
the ruler was sitting in his sun-room
looking out over his land,
when suddenly he saw
this Giant Thing
striding towards his palace.

Before he could say a word,
messengers were by his side:
'Fishermen saw it rise out of the sea.'
'Its back and belly is covered with filthy rubbish.'
'Its face is half-eaten away.'
'It crushes everything it sees.'
'It's coming this way.'

And the ruler was
terrified.

He screamed,
'Fight it. Kill it. Chop it up.'

But no one did any such thing.

Instead they ran.

They left the ruler
in his palace,
they left the ruler
too fat to move himself
fast enough.

They took his horses
they took his cars,
they took his lorries
they took his planes
and escaped.

And still the monster strode on.

CHAPTER 3

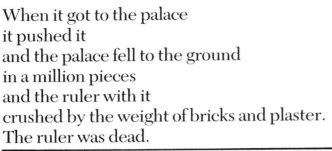

When it got to the palace
it pushed it
and the palace fell to the ground
in a million pieces
and the ruler with it
crushed by the weight of bricks and plaster.
The ruler was dead.

But this was the monster's last move.
With no smaller sea-worms
and sea-bugs to eat
tired by its journey
exhausted by its gigantic heave
to crush the palace
it lay down and died.

But the people of that land did not cheer,
they did not celebrate
they made their way towards the sea
and stood along the shore and wept.
They cried.

They said they were sorry to the sea.
They asked for the sea to forgive them.
But of course
there was no answer.

They turned to the ruler
but of course
there was no answer there either,

and so they looked to themselves
and they saw that the horses
and the cars
and the lorries
and the planes
of the ruler were now theirs.
And everything else that once
belonged to the ruler.
Now it was up to them, to decide what to do next.

And so it came about
that for the first and last time
in the history of the world
the evils of a ruler
punished the ruler himself.

No other people has ever been so lucky,
for the monsters most rulers have made
have destroyed the people first.

THE HAPPY KING

Once there was a king who was very rich and very fat. He was rich because many people worked for him, and he was fat because he ate and drank a lot. But he was quite a busy king. Every day he went out into his garden to watch his gardeners tending his strawberries and plums and peaches. Every day he went to see his weavers making his silk shirts, and every day he went to see his carpenters making his beds and tables, stairways and rafters for all his buildings.

Everywhere he went, he took with him his old friend, the Lord Chamberlain. This old friend was nearly as happy as the king – or he had to pretend, anyway, because everywhere the king went he had to sing the king's two favourite songs: *Happy days are here again*, and *God save the king*.

One day, before the fat, happy king and the Lord Chamberlain came round visiting, one of the gardeners, one of the weavers and one of the carpenters were sitting talking.

Old Jack, the gardener spoke first.

'Funny thing you know, lads, in my time I must have picked tons and tons of peaches off the peach trees in the king's fruit gardens, and do you know – I've scarcely eaten as many as would sit in these two hands.'

And then Joseph the silk weaver spoke.

'Well, I don't know about you, Jack, but I must have made enough silk in my time to stretch from here to the sea and back, and I haven't got enough plain broadcloth – let alone silk – to patch up the hole in my trousers.'

And then Nobby the carpenter spoke. 'You two can talk. Come home with me tonight, and I'll show you our most valuable belonging. A three-legged table! When we have supper, we take it in turns to be the fourth leg. I can't bear to think of the timber that went into the building of those stairs up to his bedroom.'

'I'm going to tell the king about this,' old Jack said. 'He's a good man. When he hears how hungry I've been these last few weeks, he'll understand, and he'll give us a bit more money. So Joseph, the weaver, said he would tell the king about the hole in his trousers, and Nobby said he would tell him about his three-legged table.

So that day, when the king came to the garden, up comes old Jack.

'Your Majesty,' he says.

'It's good old Jack,' the king shouted. 'How are you?'

'Not so bad, your Majesty. I was just wondering, your Majesty, if…'

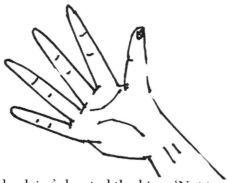

'Give him a song, Chamberlain,' shouted the king. 'Not to worry, Jack. We all wonder, we all wonder.'

The Lord Chamberlain sang *You'll never walk alone*.

'Join in, Jack,' the king said. 'It's a good old song.'

So Jack, the king and the chamberlain sang *You'll never walk alone*.

Back to work, now, Jack, my old fellow,' the king said, as he turned to the chamberlain. 'Marvellous fellow, old Jack, you know,'

Next they came to Joseph, the silk weaver.

'How's it all going, Joseph?' the king said, cheerily to old Joseph.

'Oh, not so bad, your Majesty, thanks,'

'Good, good,' the king said. 'Show us what you've done today.'

So Joseph got up and took them across to his loom, and as he went, the king saw the hole in Joseph's trousers, and he roared out laughing.

'Poor old Joseph! Do you know, Joseph, you've got a great big hole in your trousers and your bum's showing through?'

'Oh, yes,' Joseph said: I did, your Majesty, and I was going to ask you whether...whether...'

And the Lord Chamberlain started to sing.

> *Whether the weather be hot,*
> *Whether the weather be not,*
> *We'll weather the weather,*
> *Whatever the weather,*
> *Whether we like it or not.*

Then they all had a really good laugh, and Joseph went back to work.

'Marvellous old bloke, old Joseph, you know,' the king said, to the Chamberlain, and they walked on to see Nobby.

When they got to Nobby's workshop, Nobby wasn't there.

'He'll be just around the corner, I expect,' the Lord Chamberlain said.

'Well, I don't like waiting,' the king said. 'I want to see my new bed. Nobby! Nobby!'

The king shouted, but there was no answer. Nobby's coat was on the door, and Nobby's bag of tools was on the bench, so the king went over to the bench and looked in the bag. And there, in the middle of the bag, was a piece of seasoned wood. It was a piece of oak from the king's woods.

Just then, Nobby came in.

'What's this?' the king demanded.

Nobby could think of nothing to say.

'That's a... that's a... that's a hoofer-doofer... That's a thingummy-jig, your majesty.'

The happy king turned to the Chamberlain.

'What do you think it is, Chamberlain?' he said.

'It's a piece of *your* oak, your Majesty,' the Chamberlain said.

'Well, well, well,' the king said, and laughed in a nasty way. 'What a silly old fellow you are, Nobby! You tell him how silly he is, Chamberlain.'

So, the Lord Chamberlain sang a song called *You are my sunshine*, but he also took out a knife and cut off Nobby's ear.

'That's because you weren't 'ere when we arrived,' the king said. 'Next time when we call for you, you will 'ear, won't you?'

The happy king laughed at his joke, while the Chamberlain sang:

> *You are my sunshine,*
> *My only sunshine.*
> *You make me happy,*
> *When skies are grey.*
> *You'll never know dear*
> *How much I love you ...*

When he sang these last words, the Lord Chamberlain cut out Nobby's tongue.

'That's because what you said didn't make sense,' the king said.

At that, the Lord Chamberlain got ready to cut off Nobby's hand, because that's what he usually did when someone was 'handy' with the happy king's oak – the king's birds, the king's rabbits, or anything else that came out of the king's woods. But, this time, the king stopped him.

'No, Chamberlain! He can keep his hand. He'll need it to finish making my new bed. But, do finish the song, my dear fellow. We don't want to miss that.'

So the Lord Chamberlain finished his song.

...You never know, dear,
How much I love you.
Please don't take my sunshine away.

After that, the happy king and the obedient Chamberlain went off together leaving Nobby standing in the middle of his workshop with blood pouring from his head.

'Silly old Nobby,' the king said to the Chamberlain. 'Still, he'll know better next time, won't he? I mean, if I'd let him get away with that bit of wood, he'd only steal more and more, and then he'd have so much wood, he wouldn't need to work for *me* any more, would he? And then I'd have no one to make my beds and wardrobes and dressers and tables and my beautiful, beautiful chairs, would I?'

'No, your majesty, you wouldn't,' the Lord Chamberlain said, as he cleaned Nobby's blood off the royal knife. 'And what's more, your Majesty, it will be a lesson for all your other subjects to learn from.'

The king smiled happily.

'I have done good work today, Chamberlain,' he said.

'Yes, you have done good work today.' the Lord Chamberlain said.

'Justice had been done, I think, don't you, Chamberlain?'

'Justice had definitely been done, my lord,' the Lord Chamberlain said.

And they rode off, back to the palace.

As they rode off, side by side, through the fields and along the roads that led to the palace, neither the king nor the Lord Chamberlain had eyes to see the hundreds of ploughboys, bakers, maids, beggars, cowherds and dressmakers who had also received the King's Justice—just like Nobby, the carpenter. As they rode by, neither the king nor the Lord Chamberlain could hear the talk that passed between those people. And the happy king and his Chamberlain could not possibly imagine what those people were imagining: that a time would come when the King's Good Words and the King's Justice would be stopped—once and forever.